THE
HOUSE
THAT
JACK
BUILT

Poems for Shelter

THE
HOUSE
THAT
JACK
BUILT

Poems for Shelter

Edited by Brian Patten and Pat Krett

London · George Allen & Unwin Ltd
Ruskin House   Museum Street

ISBN 0 04 808014 4 hardback
       0 04 808015 2 paperback

All royalties from this book to go to Shelter

Printed in Great Britain
in 10 point Times Roman type
by Cox & Wyman Ltd,
London, Fakenham and Reading

Few people realize that one and a half million inhabited dwellings in this country are officially condemned as unfit for human habitation. Yet men, women, and children live there, as best they can. The poems in this book will give you some idea of the multiple deprivation suffered by those living in slum communities and the curbed potential of their lives. We hope that, as a result of this book, a wave of angry intolerance of this situation will gather momentum and force a solution.

There are some specific references in the book to conditions in which individual families live, drawn from Shelter's report 'Condemned', which directly inspired some of the poems.

This book stands as an indictment of a society which continues to tolerate the squalor, degradation and bitterly cruel inequality of slums.

Pat Krett, Shelter

Preface

This anthology is the result of the generous response of poets to an appeal made by Pat Krett of the St Albans Shelter Group for poems expressing the agony of slum life. But for Pat, from whom this book originated, and the St Albans group, the anthology would not have been possible.

I've made a cross-selection from the poems offered, and sought out some, already known, that I thought might add a different dimension to the book. We would like to thank all those who have contributed to this anthology, irrespective of whether or not their work is included here. Because of space and similarity between poems, many have had to be left out that we would have liked to include.

This is not 'just another anthology'. It is not 'a nice idea around which to build a collection of poems', but, we hope, a way to draw attention to the plight of those who, for the most part, go unnoticed. For it is not only the decay of houses that is involved, but a spiritual decay, an affront to the dignity of those *forced* to live in the conditions described here.

Brian Patten

Acknowledgements

Shelter, National Campaign for the Homeless, gratefully acknowledges the kind co-operation of all the poets who have contributed to this anthology, and especially those who have given Shelter copyright in their works. In addition special thanks are extended to the following publishers for permission to reprint:

Faber & Faber Ltd for 'Mr Bleaney' by Philip Larkin from *The Whitsun Weddings*, 1972: Penguin Books Ltd for 'It's a Long Time Since Anybody's Asked' from Yehuda Amichai *Selected Poems* translated into English by Assia Gutmann: Hutchinson Publishing Group Ltd for a poem by Barry McSweeney from *The Boy from the Green Cabaret Told His Mother*: The Hogarth Press and the Author's Literary Estate for 'Walls' by C. P. Cavafy translated into English by John Mavrogordato: Longman Group Ltd for 'So to Fatness Come' by Stevie Smith from *Scorpion and Other Poems*: Oxford University Press for 'Gipsies Revisited' by Derek Mahon from *Lives*, 1972; also 'Kon in Springtime' by Tony Connor from *Kon in Springtime*, 1968: Routledge & Kegan Paul Ltd for 'Brothel Allotment' by Peter Redgrove from *In the Country of the Skin*: Fulcrum Press for 'Where' and 'Labour' by Alan Jackson from *The Grim Wayfarer*, 1969; also for 'Hunga' and 'The Decadent Voyeurs' by Tom Pickard from *High on the Walls*, 1967, 1968: Jonathan Cape Ltd for 'Poem from Liverpool 8' by Adrian Henri from *Autobiography*; also 'To You That Build the New House' from Nelly Sach *Selected Poems* translated by Michael Hamburger: Latimer Press for the excerpt from Michael Horovitz extended blues poem,

Bank Holiday, 1967: Martin Secker & Warburg Ltd for 'Folding Chairs' from Günter Grass *Selected Poems* translated into English by Michael Hamburger: Migrant Press, Worcester, for 'A Worker Reads, and Asks These Questions' by Bertolt Brecht from *Sovpoems*, 1961, translated into English by Edwin Morgan: Macmillan for 'I Know it was the Place's Fault' from *The Place's Fault and Other Poems* by Philip Hobsbaum; also for 'Ode to Centre Point' by Alan Brownjohn from *Warriors Career*, 1972, which originally appeared in *Ambit*: Brunner Fact and Fiction Ltd (© 1971) for 'Fit for Human Consumption' by John Brunner (copyright ceded 1972 to Shelter by the author). And finally to Ralph Steadman for his cover illustration.

Contents

Alan Brownjohn

IN THIS CITY

In this city, perhaps a street.
In this street, perhaps a house.
In this house, perhaps a room
And in this room a woman sitting,
Sitting in the darkness, sitting and crying
For someone who has just gone through the door
And who has just switched off the light
Forgetting she was there.

Philip Larkin

MR BLEANEY

'This was Mr Bleaney's room. He stayed
The whole time he was at the Bodies, till
They moved him.' Flowered curtains, thin and frayed,
Fall to within five inches of the sill,

Whose window shows a strip of building land,
Tussocky, littered. 'Mr Bleaney took
My bit of garden properly in hand.'
Bed, upright chair, sixty-watt bulb, no hook

Behind the door, no room for books or bags –
'I'll take it.' So it happens that I lie
Where Mr Bleaney lay, and stub my fags
On the same saucer-souvenir, and try

Stuffing my ears with cotton-wool, to drown
The jabbering set he egged her on to buy.
I know his habits – what time he came down,
His preference for sauce to gravy, why

He kept on plugging at the four aways –
Likewise their yearly frame: the Frinton folk
Who put him up for summer holidays,
And Christmas at his sister's house in Stoke.

But if he stood and watched the frigid wind
Tousling the clouds, lay on the fusty bed
Telling himself that this was home, and grinned,
And shivered, without shaking off the dread

That how we live measures our own nature,
And at his age having no more to show
Than one hired box should make him pretty sure
He warranted no better, I don't know.

Yehuda Amichai

IT'S A LONG TIME SINCE ANYBODY'S ASKED

It's a long time since anybody's asked
Who lived in these houses, and who last spoke; who
Forgot his overcoat in these houses,
And who stayed. (Why didn't he run away?)

A dead tree stands among the blossoming trees.
     A dead tree.
It's an old mistake, never understood,
And at the edge of the country; the beginning
Of somebody else's time. A little silence.
And the ravings of the body and hell.
And the end of the end which moves in whispers.
The wind passed through this place
And a serious dog watched humans laugh.

Translated by Assia Gutmann

Barry McSweeney

ON THE BURNING DOWN OF THE SALVATION ARMY MEN'S PALACE, DOGS BANK, NEWCASTLE

They stood smoking damp and salvaged
cigarettes mourning their lost bundles,
each man tagged *of no fixed abode*.

Mattresses dried in the early sunshine
blankets hung over railings and gravestones
water and ashes floated across the cobbled hill.

A tinker who wouldn't give his name
bemoaned his spanner, scissors and knife-grinder,
which lay under thirty tons of debris.

Water everywhere on the steps in the dining-room
but none to make a cup of tea.

Tangled pallet frames smoked still,
men lounged around mostly in ill-fitting
borrowed clothes others naked in only
a blanket or soaked mac.

We looked at the scorched wood and remarked
how much it resembled a burnt body later we
heard it was charred corpse
we remarked how much it resembled burnt-out timber.

C. P. Cavafy

WALLS

Without consideration, without pity, without caring
They have built all around me these great high walls.

And now I can only sit here despairing.
I can think of nothing else but my fate, and the thought of it
    galls.

Because I never noticed any noise of the builders. Undes-
    cried
They have shut me up away from the world out there.

Translated by John Mavrogordato

Adrian Mitchell

MANY MANY MANY MANSIONS

(Ode on the occasion of the completion of an inter-
denominational Chaplaincy Centre at the University
of Lancaster.)

This house was built for God.
It looks good.

*'You can sit on the toilet and cook your dinner, and you
don't have to stretch out at all,' a pregnant woman told us.*

Another house for God,
In case he visits Lancaster University.

*He had come home from work to find his flat flooded with
sewage overflowing from upstairs.*

Every new house for God
Is a joke by the rich against the poor.

*'If my baby lives, the welfare may give me a place with two
bedrooms. If it dies, I'll have to stay here.'*

Every new house for God
Is a blasphemy against Mankind.

Christians and others, when you need to pray,
Go to the kitchens of the slums
Kneel to the mothers of the slums
Pray to the children of the slums

The people of the slums will answer your prayers.

Iain Crighton Smith

SPEECH FOR A POOR MAN

If God is our landlord he has left us now. . . .
Houses should be almost free, like water,
I almost said like gas, but the gas leaks.
Our houses are infested not inhabited.
The rats change sides at midnight, football teams.

And the mice grow cleverer, evade the traps.
What we come down to. . . . Once in a hotel
so many years ago, I heard a woman
complain about the thinness of the cheese. . . .
Now I go to bed early, to be warm.
For one neat room, just one, or even a bath
or some nice soap or floors that remain scrubbed!
Once I could ask for something, now I don't.
Sometimes at night I think the doorbell rings. . . .
Oftener and oftener now I hear it.

And everything is green, the scummy puddles
down from the window, the unpadlocked doors
where once there was some coal. They all forget us.
Submerged in green with ailing pumping lungs. . . .
Some day I'll manage out, perhaps in spring
and have a look at the advertisements.
Everything eats us, everything's a loss,
prices climb at night the unlit stairs. . . .
And there's no heat. I'd warm myself perhaps
by the red pictures in the Sunday Supplements.
I feed myself straight from the carrier bag.

Just once to have some money. To be warm.
To be clean and warm, in front of some nice glass.
If God is our landlord, let him make repairs.
I see his car pull off, a square of blue,
a purr of heaven, he's smoking a cigar,
brandy and trifle by his fat ringed hand. . . .

Roger McGough

OUT OF SEQUENCE

A task completed every day
Keeps sin and boredom both at bay
is what his mother used to say.

In a shop doorway
at the back of Skelhorne Street
a man in his early forties
grinning and muttering
is buttering a piece of bacon
with a pair of rusty scissors
and he has difficulty holding them
in his clumsy, larded hands.

The next day will be spent
untying the little knots

in Renshaw Street
a man with blue eyes
and skin the colour of worn pavements
burrows into the bus-stop litterbin.
The sherrybottle is empty
but there is a bacon rasher
and a screwtop foil of Lurpak,
as well as a deflated ball of string

string is great.
It ties up pillowends
and keeps the wind
out of your trouserlegs.
Things don't get lost
when there's string about.

Good to play with in bed.
Always keep some handy.

Near Windsor Street
where they are pulling down houses
there is much that rusts and glistens.
A pair of nail scissors
halfhidden by tincans, stands,
one foot in the grave.
Approaching is a man
tying a rosary of knots
into a length of dirty string.

His life, like this poem,
out of sequence,
a series of impressions,
unfinished, imperfect.

Pamela Beattie

ALONE

Yesterday you found
that on the forty-ninth square
third row up, on the left
above the mantelpiece
was a fly splat, that
wasn't there on Monday
or was it Tuesday?
You shouted 'Look'.
No one came.

Stevie Smith

SO TO FATNESS COME

Poor human race that must
Feed on pain, or choose
Another dish and hunger worse.

There is also a cup of pain, for
You to drink all up, or
Setting it aside for sweeter drink
Thirst evermore.

I am thy friend, I wish
You to sup full of the dish
I give you, and the drink,
And so to fatness come more than you think,
In health of opened heart, and know peace.

Grief spake these words to me in a dream, I thought
He spoke no more than grace allowed,
And no less than truth.

Dinos Christianopoulos

INTERVAL OF JOY

just as I was saying I would stop writing about love and lust
and write something instead about the unhappiness of my
    neighbour
I met you and fell into complete confusion
and all my resolutions went up in air

now see where I sit and write songs again
burning for your somewhat green eyes
thirsting for your saliva
recollecting our one love-walk in the country
when the mosquitoes bit us in confused bewilderment
at this incomparable devotion of ours
and the thorns pierced into our bodies
astonished at the extent of our indifference

it was an interval of joy
may the unhappy forgive me for it
I have not yet suffered enough
for the pain of my neighbour to touch me

Translated by Kimon Friar

Dinos Christianopoulos

THEY ARE TRACKING DOWN EVERYTHING PICTURESQUE

they are tracking down everything picturesque

gentlemen came with portfolios and measuring rods
they measured the ground spread out their papers
workers shooed away the pigeons
ripped up the fences tore down the house
mixed lime in the garden
brought cement raised scaffolding
they are going to build an enormous apartment house

they are wrecking the beautiful houses one by one
the houses which nourished us since we were small
with their wide windows their wooden stairs
with their high ceilings lamps on the walls
trophies of folk architecture

they are tracking down everything picturesque
chasing it away to the upper part of the town
it expires like a revolution betrayed
in a little while it will not even exist in postcards
nor in the memory or souls of our children

Translated by Kimon Friar

Ernest Frost

POSTSCRIPT FOR KURT S.

Supposing the hoard of music your life has amassed
were taken from you irrevocably,
and the flawless silence of your walk through the early
       mornings
were denied. Supposing that your children, picking
the raspberries up in the wood that hangs
over the face of the mountain, were not to delight
in their day of high altitudes, of danger, of
perfumed fruit. Supposing your wife
with her slide and straight hair – the plain girl
with her elbows always in flour – gave up
her baking and preserves, and your bare bright house began
to lose its smell of bread: that there grew
a new black smell, sickened and dense.
If this were so, perhaps I would come
on the midnight train, in my long overcoat
chilled with the winter, come to enquire,
abashed and ashamed for you, and mourn for a life
denied its music and work and children.
Yes, and the yellow bird in the cage, with the faces
smiling up at it and telling it histories
of hanging gardens, and the picture by the man
who spoke each day to the famous composer. . . .
Supposing this came to an end.

Supposing instead you came into these places
and we had to discard our suits of words and had
no feelings to replace them, for feelings, too, had fled
except the huge cloud of perplexity, and then
supposing we sat down and laid our heads
silently weeping on the board by the sink

and saw the day depart from us, the night descend
laden with parcels of small dirty dreams
coming apart, and waking in the night to find the room
foetid, swollen with recriminations, bleeding
away between the legs, unstaunched, unblessed,
broken and beaten down, unblessed, unblessed. . . .

Derek Mahon

GIPSIES REVISITED
(for Julian Harvey)

Sorry, gippos – I have
watched the dark police
rocking your caravans
to wreck the crockery
and wry thoughts of peace
you keep there on waste
ground beside motorways
where the snow lies late
and am ashamed – fed,
clothed, housed and ashamed.
You might be interested
to hear, though, that on
stormy nights our strong
double glazing groans with
foreknowledge of death,
the fridge with a great wound,
and not surprised to know
the fate you have so long
endured is ours also,
the cars are piling up.
I listen to the wind
and file receipts. The heap
of scrap metal in my
garden grows daily.

Peter Redgrove

BROTHEL ALLOTMENT

The house where the smoke from the chimneys is as red
as blood.
The woman in the house who is also the floor: her dress
flows into her long skirt which weaves into the carpet.
The old man in the kitchen who is also the oven.
The young woman of the house who enters from the
drains, wearing green.
The young lad who visits, smelling of grass-cuttings.
The meal of appleseeds served.
The hot petrol drunk.
The stairs that are the keys of the piano that musics
them upstairs.
The bed that is an inlet of the sea.
The covers that are white and salt and the bedlight that
goes down red.
The awakening to gulls and sleet.
The breakfast of loose change.
The street home that is a well.

Traditional

THE HOUSE THAT JACK BUILT

This is the house that Jack Built.

This is the bread
That lay in the house that Jack built.

This is the rat
That ate the bread
That lay in the house that Jack built.

This is the cat
That killed the rat
That ate the bread
That lay in the house that Jack built.

This is the dog
That worried the cat
That killed the rat
That ate the bread
That lay in the house that Jack built.

This is the boy with the crumpled face
That kicked the dog
That worried the cat
That killed the rat
That ate the bread
That lay in the house that Jack built.

This is the maiden all forlorn
Who loved the boy with the crumpled face
Who kicked the dog
That worried the cat

That killed the rat
That ate the bread
That lay in the house that Jack built.

This is the man all tattered and torn
Who fathered the maiden all forlorn
Who loved the boy with the crumpled face
Who kicked the dog that worried the cat
That killed the rat that ate the bread,
That lay in the house that Jack built.

This is the wife without any hope
Who clung to the man all tattered and torn
Who fathered the maiden all forlorn
Who loved the boy with the crumpled face
Who kicked the dog that worried the cat
That killed the rat that ate the bread
That lay in the house that Jack built.

And this is the mess at the end of it all,
This is the mess in which they all fall,
Poor people all confused and forlorn
Because of the house that Jack built.

Bill Pickard

OMNIBUS SHELTER

Build me a prison
For these grown-up boys.
A hard heartbreaking place
To tone them down.

Build me a prison –
Well away from town.

Raise a Remand Home
For these teenage tarts
Whose hateful eyes
Express their hateful hearts.

Raise a Remand Home.
That's what I advise.

Haven't they Hostels
To lay down their heads,
And Children's Homes
To lay a life's foundation?

Haven't they Hostels
Paid for by the nation?

Vast empty Business Blocks
Shall surely rise.
Manna came down
From those encumbered skies.

Non nobis domine. A shack, pro tem.
Non nobis domine. Not us. But them.

Paul Ableman

ANOTHER STORY

I am not too concerned about homes,
(The mere frame of life). I am more concerned
About how to rescue the future from the past
And how to light the flares so that man
May one day land safely at his destiny.
I am concerned about love
And the cultivation of love
By new and old gardening techniques
So that it will spread and flourish
Throughout the planet. I am concerned
About polishing the lens of the imagination
So that it will be bright and clear
And able to ignite
The flame of art.
No, I am not too concerned about homes –
But then I have a home!
It is warm, clean, spacious-enough and has
A splendid view.
If I were homeless, or coughed in a slum,
It would be another story.

Edwin Morgan

TWO GLASGOW SONNETS

I

A mean wind wanders through the back-court trash.
Hackles on puddles rise, old mattresses
puff briefly and subside. Play-fortresses
of brick and bric-a-brac spill out some ash.

Four storeys have no windows left to smash,
but in the fifth a chipped sill buttresses
mother and daughter the last mistresses
of that black block condemned to stand, not crash.

Around them the cracks deepen, the mice crawl.
The kettle whimpers on a crazy hob.
Roses of mould grow from ceiling to wall.

The man lies late since he has lost his job,
smokes on one elbow, letting his coughs fall
thinly into an air too poor to rob.

II

'See a tenement due for demolition?
I can get ye rooms in it, two, okay?
Seven hundred and nothing legal to pay
for it's no legal, see? That's my proposition,

ye can take it or leave it but. The position
is simple, you want a hoose, I say
for eight hundred pound it's yours.' And they,
trailing five bairns, accepted his omission

of the foul, crumbling stairhead, windows wired
not glazed, the damp from the canal, the cooker
without pipes, packs of rats that never tired –

any more than the vandals bored with snooker
who stripped the neighbouring houses, howled, and fired
their aerosols – of squeaking 'Filthy lucre! '

Alec Reid

LIFE AT NUMBER NINE

The television in its prissy corner
Removed its picture at a peak hour
The wife expected sex.
The man stared in disbelief,
Not at her.
His stomach's weight above him
Rolled him sideways from the chair.
He crawled whimpering to the screen,
Pressed his nose against it, waiting.
Nothing.
Detaching with a damp patch
He grunted upright,
Straining unaccustomed ankles,
Noticed the draught from the curtained window,
The bleakness in furniture.
No picture.
He kicked the bloody thing
To make it go
As if it were a donkey
In some fairy tale
Many years ago.

Alan Jackson

CITY MAN

the soaring inequity
the tumble down might
the striding dwarf
the city man
the plague dweller
the endemic rat
home to illness
and away to fuck
the lamplit scarperer
the denizen of brick
a hundred pleasures at his twiddle tips

and the memory of one sunny holiday up his nose
'they let us out of the bus
and i got a snap of the river'

are we bleeding millions
white to dying with riding our handbags
a race?
more like a bloody rush
more like a kid's sweetie bag
of manufactured muck
burst on the ground
and we
sneaky ratbags
of tenement and terminal
what memories we cherish
what fond tales we'll pass on
of struggles in the sun and wind
and possibly drizzles in the late afternoon

Alan Jackson

THWARTED

I live forlorn on the seventh floor
of a corporation flat
which the children all have fell from
and the pigeons have beshat

I do not mind the loneliness
the long evenings with the tellie
but I do wish the wind hadn't altered the flight
of the brick I dropped on Jock Kelly

Alan Jackson

WHERE

apple cake distributed
    between the poor
not one asking
excuse me,
where
          do these apples
grow?

Henry Graham

GOOD LUCK TO YOU KAFKA/ YOU'LL NEED IT BOSS

the man from the finance company
came again today he wants to know
when i'm going to pay but what he won't say
is what it was i bought

one morning perhaps when i was high
on poetry and corned jock butties
i must have wandered threepartsmental
into a department store and bought something

a three-piece suite for my sweet
a frigidaire to keep frozen my despair
a fitted carpet for the inside of my head

he just won't say what it was
and when i laugh he looks the other way
apparently i have only fourteen days left
he won't even say what happens then

i suppose they will come and take away my eyes
(which i know i haven't paid for)
or the words that live inside my head
or my surprise at raindrops or the use

of my legs or my love of bread
then again they just might forget
about me and go away/fat chance

Henry Graham

POEM IN AID OF FLIES
(Liverpool 8 1970)

Making a poem in the face of this crumbling decay
is an obscene travesty, a miscarriage.
Yet make a poem I must;
a desperate attempt to atone, a compromise.

Looking out of this window not a roof
seems intact. A little old woman
with a large brown dog lives in a small back room;
and when I hang my head out of the window
the dog shouts its amazement, and decrepit
broken kings on ruined roofs laugh and topple
their dingy crowns into the dirty back yards.
The whore with the orange wings sings me a dreary ditty
as she floats down the paper strewn street
three feet
off the pavement.
Sad short time angel, yearning to fly
higher and higher, away from the kneetrembling
fear of being passed by in favour of golf.

We have just removed the light fitting
from the centre of the room, but the flies
still circle there hoping it's only temporary.
How long will you eliminate their patient searching
with that death ray spray
you wield with such relish?
And how long shall the words of your mouth
be like an empty wind?

Maureen Duffy

CONDEMNED

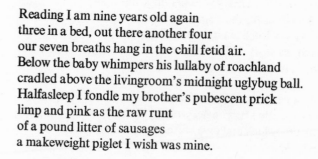

Reading I am nine years old again
three in a bed, out there another four
our seven breaths hang in the chill fetid air.
Below the baby whimpers his lullaby of roachland
cradled above the livingroom's midnight uglybug ball.
Halfasleep I fondle my brother's pubescent prick
limp and pink as the raw runt
of a pound litter of sausages
a makeweight piglet I wish was mine.

We live by bread almost alone
with jam on it. Dinners bubble and squeak
their second or third time round.
The morning kettle is filled with eskimo splinters
that dewdrop the tap in the yard.
Hot yellow streams splash back from the rinked pan
while the draught under the door manacles
grimy ankles from across steppes of allotment.

So close it seems in the sour smell
from these pages, wounds scarred over by thirty years
bleed as at the approach of murderers.
Still I am childishly impotent to make
one least change in a life so like
the opening of mine. They are slaughtering
innocents with charity Christmas stockings
over their faces garnished with gold coins
of bitter chocolate and foil.

Like nightmares we can't pin them down
lash them to the wormy bedfoot, the crevassed
floorboard, spreadeagle them over the colander roof.
I hear Herod's soldiery in the street
calling for a young throat to whet
their razor edge. Heavy with her majority
Democracy stalks the slums, her liberty cap
shadowing a witch hat on the crumbling walls
for bedtime story. While reason nods
she too is mother to monsters.

Child on page 31, area crowned and barred
only Desperate Dan can get you out of there,
I came up by luck and love and all I can throw you
is this frayed rope of twisted words.

Pat Waites

WHY THE HELL DUMP TRUCK

the engines are moving to wake the day
That's one thing about the twentieth century
you can depend on a little pre-drawn resonance
                    even on the farm
as if in these winter hours to chide the tardy sun
Why not rip up the municipal carpark
                    with a couple of pneumatic drills
it's only a suggestion
but if we really got down to it
we could have holes everywhere

Marjorie Baldwin

COMING HOME

'I was always far out
And not waving, but drowning.' Stevie Smith

My cat came home.
He smelt like a line of clean washing,
His paws bore the scent of forest moss,
Of countless secret hunting places,
Where water ran and twigs cracked,
And silence laughed.
He demanded supper with delight,
Then washed his feet one by one,
and curled up on the sofa.

Her child came home.
The smell was so bad that he stayed in the street,
(It was summertime, when smells are worst).
He ate his bread and jam on the kerb.
He did not wash.
He stayed there till the rats came out.
Rapt by their sudden moves and furtive eyes
He watched them turn over the rotten scraps,
And find the poison – while my cat slept.

What is this human race? this tribe of gods?
Ordained such living space – such nourishment?
The Town Hall cuts the losses for us all,
While plans proliferate, computers hum.
The goal on this road is the single end –
And there humanity both waves and drowns.

Hugh Lauder

TRIAL

I sit by the window; beside me,
the child's pastel eyes
staring widely through the glass.

Behind me the woman
sits at her dressing table
combing her hair
the beat is five brushes to the minute.
With each stroke she stops to examine herself;
this morning her eyebrows are heavy
crossed upon the forehead.

Outside three wood pigeons
on a branch
at right angles to a yew.
Puffed up with snow beneath their wings
grotesque in their proportions
sitting strictly upon the bough;
the wind rocks it gently.

At this distance they stare
as one eye
impartial, unnerving.

Three judges sizing up this room.
Behind me the woman paces up and down
advocate for the prosecution.
The child,
                victim.

Michael Stevens

COMING HOME

She comes back to the room that she calls home.

We
Blame the blind architect
For the broken stairs.

We
Curse the quick builder
For the climbing damp.

We
Happily rebuke the Housing Department
For the homelessness.

She
Dreams of sleeping through
The derelict tomorrow –
Cancel out this crowded space
Where washing hangs damply along the walls
And water cannot clean –
For ever forget this agony
And dream of sleeping on.

We
See only those
Facades that flake forwards on delicate balustrades.

But she
Must always come back to the room that she calls home.

Nelly Sach

TO YOU THAT BUILD THE NEW HOUSE

'There are stones like souls.' Rabbi Nachman

When you come to put up your walls anew –
Your stove, your bedstead, table and chair –
Do not hang your tears for those who departed,
Who will not live with you then,
On to the stone.
Nor on the timber –
Else weeping will pierce the sleep,
The brief sleep you have yet to take.

Do not sigh when you bed your sheets,
Else your dreams will mingle
With the sweat of the dead.

Oh, the walls and household utensils
Are responsive as Aeolian harps
Or like a field in which your sorrow grows,
And they sense your kinship with dust.

Build, when the hourglass trickles,
But do not weep away the minutes
Together with the dust
That obscures light.

Translated by Michael Hamburger

Reprinted from the *Penguin Book Of Socialist Verse*

Michael Horovitz

CHORUS #31 FROM BANK HOLIDAY

. . . Tomorrow
you're open – so
why don't you stay wide open –
stay on holiday *every* day

And yield your sway
to the little man who made you –
who plays today and pays
with bombs in your fireless image

Yield both O powers give over
to yon bonny banks and braes
celestial flowers on earth
before you and hereafter

Today
H-bombs pronounce you bankrupt
and yet the sun shines bright
Sobeit! Bankrupt be –
Explode your nowhere pledges –
Burn up your nothing statements –
Release your no-body staffs –
Open up your golden vaults for
who wants to play Monopoly –

On your cornerstones of bonded civic pride
I slough my hermit hide
so tired of toiling
remembering Zion
I lie down
and weep

for my journey
for true love
for you –
Babel towers above

scraping the charter'd sky
blocking free passage
on low roads and high

only God can pass you by

> – *For thus saith the* LORD:
> *Ye were sold for nought:*
> *And ye shall be redeemed without money* ...

– modern man endorses his cheque
to lose his own way
and follow the dinosaur down ...

Ivor Cutler

GORBALS 1930

The message
boy had green snot running
down his nose.
Granny Goldberg
gave him a big green
cooker.
Snot flowed
over the
sharply-defined upper
lip onto the sharp bitten apple.
Brown teeth on white tart
flesh.
Uncle Joe shared
a lavvy with seven families
on a steep circular staircase.
I went
in with the steel key.
The bowl was all
diarrhoea and choked newspaper.
It
was
strangers' diarrhoea.

I decided to wait.

Brian Patten

INTERRUPTION AT THE OPERA HOUSE

At the very beginning of an important symphony,
while the rich and famous were settling into their quietly
    expensive boxes,
a man came crashing through the crowds
carrying in his hand a cage in which
the rightful owner of the music sat,
yellow and tiny and very poor.
And taking onto the rostrum this rather timid bird
he turned up the microphone, and it sang.

'A very original beginning to the evening,' murmured the
    crowds,
quietly glancing at their programmes to find
the significance of the intrusion.

Meanwhile at the box office, the organizers of the evening
were arranging for small and uniformed attendants
to evict, even forcefully, the intruders.
But as the attendants, poor and gathered from the nearby
    slums at little expense,
went rushing down the aisles to do their job,
they heard above the coughing and irritable rattle of jewels
a sound that filled their heads with light.
And from somewhere inside them bubbled up a stream,
and there came a breeze on which their youth was carried.
How sweetly the bird sang!

And though soon the furwrapped crowds were leaving their
    boxes
and in confusion were winding their ways home,
still the attendants sat in the aisles,
and some, so delighted with what they heard, rushed out to
call their families and friends.

And their children came,
sleepy for it was late in the evening,
and they hardly knew if they'd done with dreaming
or had begun again.

In all the tenement blocks
the lights were clicking on,
and the rightful owner of the music,
tiny but no longer timid sang
for the rightful owners of the song.

D

Günter Grass

FOLDING CHAIRS

How sad these changes are.
People unscrew the name plates from the doors,
take the saucepan of cabbage
and heat it up again, in a different place.

What sort of furniture is this
that advertises departure?
People taking up their folding chairs
and emigrate.

Ships laden with homesickness and the urge to vomit
carry patented seating contraptions
and unpatented owners
to and fro.

Now on both sides of the great ocean
they are folding chairs;
how sad these changes are.

Translated by Michael Hamburger

Harold Massingham

DERELICTION

Something's rotten in the state of dwellings –
in all these slum package-deals, tenements, multi-lets,
    terraces:
they're the scabies of England,
the itch of cities.

Dereliction's at home –
in fact he enjoys the filthy sadness in the air:
it's good for his diarrhoea, gut-rot, his itch and leaking
    pustules,
and the rats he breeds.

Dereliction's laugh is the thwack of ceiling-plaster,
dereliction's smirk is a gas-leak,

dereliction pisses down the walls,
a greening urine,
dereliction won't be decorated, he rejects wallpaper like
    healing poultices,

dereliction hangs round the houses,
dereliction sits on door-steps
with sticky knickers,
with a hopeless wariness,

dereliction sits on kitchen-beds with the mute faces of
    19th-century street-children,
dereliction is motherhood
full of nerve-pills,
fatherhood
brutal or numb.

Something is rotten in the state of dwellings,
something is rotten in the state,
something is rotten –

dereliction is the human junk-bin,
the mini-Collective,

these photographs of untenable disgrace.

Jack Clemo

THE FROSTED IMAGE

Crude designs are mildewed on a huddle of walls,
Explored by vermin and cynical snails
In the dark hours when the unripe dreamer
Is jarred by an adjoining growl of mature heat;
And high above them sometimes space-men soar,
Moon-bound, sleeping in turns as they mount,
Smiling at the obsolete slum child,
The bud of gunman and whore,
Far back, surely frosted,
Down there on the advanced planet.

In my own cramped room I have said
That a true vision flowers undaunted
By rats' reek and sodden paper.
I have pointed to Bernadette
Racing to her Lady, blithe in the dawn-flare,
Retrieved from the motions on the straw bed
And the lice clotting her hair.

But the saint's view is rare, seeming of small account
When men circle so high to bestride
Dead space where open breath is denied –
Science shedding an astral glamour
That mocks the clammy sore, the laggard place
Where design and breeding breath lack space.

Bertolt Brecht

A WORKER READS, AND ASKS
THESE QUESTIONS

Who built Thebes with its seven gates?
In all the books it says kings.
Did kings drag up those rocks from the quarry?
And Babylon, overthrown time after time
Who built it up again as often? What walls
In dazzling gilded Lima house the builders?
When evening fell on the completed wall of China
Where did the stone-masons go? Great Rome
Is thick with triumphal arches. Who erected them? Who
    was it
The Caesars triumphed over? Had famous Byzantium
Nothing but palaces, where did the people live? Atlantis
    itself,
The drowning roaring for their slaves.

The young Alexander took India.
By himself?
Caesar hammered Gaul.
Had he not even a cook beside him?
Philip of Spain cried as his fleet
Foundered. Did no one else cry?
Frederick the Second won the Seven Year War. Who
Won it with him?

Someone wins on every page.
Who cooked the winner's banquet?
One great man every ten years.
Who paid the expenses?

So many statements.
So many questions.

Translated by Edwin Morgan

Philip Hobsbaum

I KNOW IT WAS THE PLACE'S FAULT

Once, after a rotten day at school –
Sweat on my fingers, pages thumbed with smears,
Cane smashing down to make me keep them neat –
I blinked out to the sunlight and the heat
And stumbled up the hill, still swallowing tears.
A stone hissed past my ear – 'Yah! gurt fat fool!'

Some urchins waited for me by my gate.
I shouted swear-words at them, walked away.
'Yeller', they yelled, ' 'e's yeller!' And they flung
Clods, stones, bricks – anything to make me run.
I ran, all right, up hill all scorching day.
With 'yeller' in my eyes. 'I'm not, I'm not!'

Another time, playing too near the shops –
Oddly, no doubt, I'm told I was quite odd,
Making, no doubt, a noise – a girl in slacks
Came out and told some kids 'Run round the back,
Bash in his back door, smash up his back yard,
And if he yells I'll go and fetch the cops.'

And what a rush I had to lock those doors
Before that rabble reached them! What desire
I've had these twenty years to lock away
That place where fingers pointed out my play,
Where even the grass was tangled with barbed wire,
Where through the streets I waged continual wars!

We left (it was a temporary halt)
The knots of ragged kids, the wired-off beach, behind
the blinds. I'll not return;
There's nothing there I haven't had to learn,
And I've learned nothing that I'd care to teach –
Except that I know it was the place's fault.

55

Robert Shaw

INSIDE GREAT LONDON

*'Inside the Soviet Union political and other dissenters are
sent to places like Siberia. In post-revolutionary society the
managers still manage and the poor are still poor and
oppressed.'*

Comrade Sergei, during my visit
To Great London I took every
Opportunity to discover more
About The Penal Settlement
To The North, of which we hear
So many rumours. It appears
Its name is a word for whispers.
Only rarely is it used in public
And then always the custom
Is for the speaker over his right
Shoulder to throw it – whether from
Superstition or against contamination
I do not know. What is certain
Is that you cannot go there.
You must always be sent.
Political reasons are often
Conjectured for such transportations,
In private, of course, though
Lack of sociability is also
A common cause – sociologists
Note dwellers in the zone are morose
And sullen. Up there, one may also
Find second- and third-generation
Dwellers, 'Narffeners', as they are

Called, their ancestors being among
The First Sent, to work The Mines after
The Revolution. These Originals
Inhabit gruesome tenements
Known as 'The Backs', close to places
Of work, so few man-hours are lost.
There being no Weather up there,
They are, for the most part, silent.
Their children, it seems, require
Only the most rudimentary instruction,
Happily for The Economy.
'Signs being taken for wonders',
As The Great Londoner poet says,
The natives are greatly moved by
Great London elections to select
Those who will do more for the Great
And less for the rest.
Fortunately for the regime,
Narffeners' memories are short
And they continue to take rituals
For their further restrainment
With all seriousness.
One would think such backward
Pockets better abandoned. Nevertheless,
The Great assure us, this tiny
Corner for the feckless and dirty
Is vitally necessary
For their prosperity.

Alan Bold

LIFE CLASS

AND NOW: an experiment you can observe
Under local conditions. It is called
    'CREATING A PROBLEM'.

Take two people. Let them love each other.
Let them also have the opportunity to indulge
Their love. The result is likely to be
One or more new human beings.
Whatever happens they will need
Somewhere to live as well as
Somewhere to love.

Having created the initial situation
Watch closely how the arbitrary human group
Reacts to difficulties – which we will provide.

Let the difficulties be:
        houses that emit foul odours
        houses that are shared by rodents
    houses that seep with damp
houses that tend to fall to bits.

In short, ensure that their dwellings
Constantly impinge on the consciousness
Of the group under observation.

In these perfect test conditions
Members of the group will begin to resent
One another. There may even be violence,
Rising like the damp,
Beginning with shrill hysterical screams, and
Ending in increasingly destructive

                              physical
                              gestures.
They will, in fact, begin to hurt each other.

Should you develop this further
By introducing a sudden loss of employment
You will have constructed a classic case
of induced squalor leading to neurotic tension
And finally breaking down into all sorts of
      Despair.

The problem has, thus, been successfully created.

AND NOW: Who will volunteer a solution?

Dave Cunliffe

AND MAYBE IF OUR BLINKERS
SLIP A BIT

Didn't we search each forest morning
for food and clothing; before embracing
caves of night for warmth and shelter.

Didn't we join with tribal hunters.
Share spoils of fruitful gatherers.
Celebrate open communal feasts.

So, which of us thought up slum ghettos.
Grim streets of sad and lonely dying rooms.
Stink of dust and grime; despair, decay.

Who keeps on shoving people into a mess
so sticky, it hurts to crawl away:
as if bees grew fat on soured jam.

And maybe if our blinkers slip a bit.
And granite ears turn towards new winds.
And indifferent restraining hands unclaw. . . .

John Brunner

FIT FOR HUMAN CONSUMPTION

Air: Traditional, 'Come All Ye Tramps and Hawking Lads'

Of all the jobs in Eng-a-land the landlord's is the best –
He takes our money and drinks his wine and lays him down
    to rest.
He lies between his satin sheets in a bed that's warm and dry,
And his sleep is sound for the walls around shut out my
    baby's cry.
There are fleas and rats in these filthy flats and the toilet's
    sprung a leak,
But the landlord cares for the stocks and shares our rent will
    buy next week.

I went to see the landlord and I acted most polite,
I told him of the rats and fleas that plague us every night.
He poured me full of whisky and he sent me home by car,
And he raised my rent twenty-five per cent to help re-stock
    his bar.
For the landlord's house never saw a mouse, let alone a rat
    or flea –
I believe he thinks that our leaks and stinks are all imagin'ry!

We had to have the doctor, and he came around to call.
We showed him broken windows and the fungus on the wall,
We showed him pools of water, showed him dry-rot in the
    floor,
And he said we should have it all made good for that's
    against the law,
But we'd best be quick as the kid was sick and he mustn't
    catch a chill –
That was months ago for the law is slow and the baby's
    coughing still.

There's sewage draining down the wall behind the kitchen
    sink –
Make all the laws you like to make and sewage still will stink!
I went to tell the council, but the mayor cried, 'Police!
The landlord swears he can't make repairs, he rang me up
    from Nice! '
Oh, they gave me bail, but I'd rather jail, it might help to save
    my health,
For I tell you this, that the shit and piss are fertilising
    wealth!

I want to lay the landlord down in the bed I have to use,
I want the damp to rot his clothes, the mould to foul his
    shoes,
I want to see him shiver, want to hear his chattering teeth,
Join him in the queue for the only loo where the pee drips
    out beneath,
Feed him chips and beans and a pan of greens instead of
    coq au vin,
Let him smell disease every time he breathes and see how
    long he can!

Adrian Henri

POEM FOR LIVERPOOL 8

Liverpool 8
blaze of trumpets from basement recordplayers
loud guitars in the afternoon
knowing every inch of little St Bride St
brightgreen patches of mildew redpurple bricks stained
    ochre plaster
huge hearts names initials kisses painted on backdoors
tiny shop with a lightbulb in the window
Rodney St pavement stretching to infinity
Italian garden by the priest's house
seen through the barred doorway on Catherine St
pavingstones worn smooth for summer feet
St James Rd my first home in Alan's flat
shaken intolerably by Cathedral bells on Sundays
Falkner Sq. Gardens heaped with red leaves to kick in
    autumn
shuttered yellowgreen with sunlight
noisy with children's laughter in summer
black willows into cold mist
bushes railings pillowed with snow in winter
Gambier Terrace loud Beatle guitars hiding behind painted
    words bright colours
in the flooded catfilled basement
pigeons disappearing at eyelevel into the mist
hopscotch-figures vomit-stains under my morning feet
Granby St bright bazaars for aubergines and coriander
Blackburne Place redbrick Chirico tower rushing back after
    noon
Blackburne Place redbrick Chirico tower rushing back after
    love at dinnertime
drunk jammed in the tiny bar in The Cracke

drunk in the crowded cutglass Philharmonic
drunk in noisy Jukebox O'Connor's
smiling landlord on the doorstep huge in shirtsleeves and
    braces
now a wasteland
murdered by planners not German bombers
crossed by empty roads
drunken lintels falling architraves
Georgian pediments peeling above toothless windows
no Mrs Boyne laughing in the Saturdaynight Greek chipshop
the tumbledown graveyard under the Cathedral
where we kissed behind willowtrees
bulldozed into tidy gardens
huge tornup roots of trees
pink sandstone from uprooted walls glittering in pale sun-
    light
no happy dirtyfaced children
littering the sidestreets
only a distant echo of their laughter
across the bonfire fire-engine debris.

George Barker

THE CHILDREN AT MY DOOR

The children at the door
the children worlds away
all knock upon my one
and only heart this day
and in the hallowed evening
I hear the bright stars cry
and dance about like children
in the October sky.

Where are the stars at morning
and the bright children gone?
Here in my hearts of hearts
children and stars dance on.
In the red sky of morning
I feel about my soul
the stars and children dancing
as round a starry pole.

E

George Mackay Brown

POEM

Who was so rich
He owned diamonds and oil and fire,
The leaf and the forest,
Herring and whale and horizon –
Who had the key to the chamber beyond the stars
And the key of the grave –
Who was sower and seed and bread
Came on a black night
To a poor hovel with a star peeping through the rafters,
And slept among beasts
And put a sweet cold look on kings and shepherds.

But the children of time, their rooftrees should be strong.

Pamela Zinnemann

HAMMER

you and i began to build a house.
the plot of ground happened upon us,
we did not expect to find it
or to have it given to us,
nor had we thought
to build a house together, you and i.
the plans we drew were good
and solid: and, more important,
pleasing to the eye;
the work commenced quickly
and with feverish
activity, and from the foundations
grew the walls and the divisions;
and dream shapes were built
in solid forms.

and then one day i slept in the house
before it was finished
and so you took a hammer
and began to hack away until
the bricks began to crumble
and with determination you found other implements
to crack the walls and the divisions
until they tottered
and the house collapsed.
'hard work is good work' you said
as you went to the trouble of working
to smash the forms and contours of our building,
and then, with satisfaction, you said,
'a good worker always stands firmly on solid ground'
and with satisfaction you walked away from the house of
    rubble.

Tom Pickard

HUNGA

Theres a pain in my stomach called hunga
it happens six days of the week
on friday wi gan t'the assistance
thi give us some money to seek
and to see some way of payin wa way
some way of payin wa way
fora day
some way of payin wa way

On monday wi gan wi oot bacon
on tuesday wi gan wi oot meat
on wednesday wi gan wi oot bread
on thursday wi gits nowt ti eet
on friday aa gans an aa begs

Theres a pain in my stomach called hunga
it happens six days of the week
on friday wi gan t'the assistance
thi give us some money to seek
and to see some way of payin wa way
some way of payin wa way
fora day
some way of payin wa way

Av not got the money ti buy her new clothes
av not got the money to buy him some toys
al not git me hair cut
al not git a job
as rather be skint than an industrial cog

Theres a pain in my stomach called hunga
it happens six days of the week
on friday wi gan t'the assistance
thi give us some money to seek
and to see some way of payin wa way
some way of payin wa way
fora day
some way of payin wa way

Thi send a inspecta roond
each day of the week
ti see if am lookin for work,
but av got me coat on
an walkin the toon
forst tryin to borro a short.

Theres a pain in my stomach called hunga
it happens six days of the week
on friday wi gan t'the assistance
thi give us some money to seek
and to see some way of payin wa way
some way of payin wa way
fora day
some way of payin wa way

Tom Pickard

THE DECADENT VOYEURS

They pass factories and pits and poverty
in flashy cars, and spit;
and return to coal warm fires
which from the earth
these other men have ripped.

Alan Brownjohn

ODE TO CENTRE POINT

One of the most
Paradoxical of infertil
-ity symbols
Lately contrived, a vast
Barren phallus of
Egg-boxes without eggs, it
Simultaneously wav
-ers and maintains its own
Projection into the
Soft depths of the sky, a
Thing of monumental
Insignificance, making no
Impression and
Quite ignorable, unless for
Its huge vac
-uity. But in so rapidly
Appearing, it rased out
Everything lively on its site:
Small blocks of
Usefully inhabited mansion
Flats, various
Helpful shops, passable
Ristorante, an
Experimental theatre, and
All of the navigable
Pavement on one side of the
Charing Cross Road,
Substituting, at ground level, a
Blue pond inside
Crass concrete walls with square

-Fingered fountains jetting
The water; and above, shooting upward
        A weird, implacable
Cliff of patterned stone, glass and
        Air, a hive of empty
Cells, tilting, apparently, as the
        Clouds above pass over,
And at one dizzying, approximate
        Count, thirty-three stories high.
Therefore, it impinges on us all,
        Notwithstanding, and needs
To be taken into account; which
        Is why strong men with de
-termination and research have
        Gone grey trying to
Discover why it is there
        (But then who, exactly,
Wanted and actually willed Shell
        Mex or the Euston Road?)
– And what it is to do? Such
        A thing is like the
Clothes without the Emperor,
        Flaunting what looks like
Purpose in order to cover weakness
        And chaos, proving again
That somehow, in our time, all
        Towers are peculiarly
Bad, contraptions of antisense,
        Contraceptions of truth,
And things which one day might,
        With the clarity of simply
Looking at what is there, be just taken
        Down and scrapped. Indeed,
What couldn't we do when even
        The few square yards on
Which we base giant follies were
        Fruitful and even

Innocent again, with perfectly
            Natural weeds? To
Have one as a play-space for
            Technocrats to
Run around and play utterly
            Virginal games of Bank Robbers on,
Instead of the real thing,
            Might be a splendid
Idea for its owner to install
            If he ever repented
Of the tremendous non-use to which
            He put one quarter
-acre of our possible grass. And
            Perhaps one damn good
Roundabout with small, wry,
            Cynical horses' faces to
Ride on, going perpetually grinning
            Round and round would be,
Though futile, a bit more sense.

                            Mean

            -while, until the world
Turns thus inconceivably pure
            And benevolent, the whole thing
Will rear up in front of the eye,
            Narrowing into the heavens and
Widening at its base like some
            -thing unnatural and
Unmotivated found one morning
            In any man's life, and
Probably the result of some
            Nasty and unremembered
Dream.
                    Well, in a way, I'd hate
            -With its uniformed toughs, trained
Alsatians and all, to knock it down
            And spoil anyone's happy
Fantasies, an act for which I may

72

Have no moral right after
So much indulgence of my own,
    But . . . one's most citizenly
Sort of impatience sometimes rises,
    Just as suddenly,
It lugged with it some uncitizenly
    Substance which might go
Off, and reasoning: Reality ought to be
    -gin somewhere, so why not
With somebody else, who has thirty-two
    Stories less of it than me?

Alan Jackson

LABOUR

the black makes the black black
the black makes the black black
the black makes the black black

the world grows round in orange whorls

its smithereens are held together
by toil by care
sweat of the ox
makes the glue
for casing robots

inside not delicate machinery
inside not warm wet
inside
one spring one clock one bomb

the symbol of labour is a fist
yes
the symbol of labour is a punch
yes
the symbol of labour is a hard knot
a thwart
a dam
a detonation

and the labouring man is black
at heart

David Gill

THE USES OF POVERTY

Yes, I love Dickens best:
those characters soaring like sixpenny rockets
above their walled back-yards,
those bumbling, twisting, dodging times
in the great rat-town of London
where the fat and squeezing prosperous
taxed the very sun
and brought on blindness
in the windows of the poor.
I know, I know,
for every character that rose
and shone in a diaspora of stars
ten died and in cheap coffins found
a pauper's grave.

But what of those who live today
beneath damp ceilings mapped with scabs,
and next to walls whose brick ribs jut
through broken skin:
the borough-poor, the hostel-folk
bed-sitting the ill-lit hours
until the silver-gulping gas-fire dies
and sleep divests them of
their threadbare circumstances
in which they shrink
defeated?

Why, give them time: their squalor too
some genius will render fine.
Meanwhile, just give me Dickens,
Dickens every time.

S. K. Smith

THE BOX

This boy keeps dreams in a box,
Blue shirt, two books and a card
For one dead birthday, three years out of date.

Nothing can make him cry,
Now he is ten:
Not callous cold, not damp,
Not skin worn raw.

Guarding his box from rats,
Whose teeth taste crusts and dreams alike
Indifferently,
He sleeps on edge, night's vermin on the sill;
He sleeps in a box, four walls, five children breathing,
Packed in each other's whispers.

Only this box will carry home his name,
Imprinted barely on a tattered label.
Christopher Robin. Chaucer House.
With care.

Nina Steane

SEMIDETACHED

Lying in bed,
he hears rotting beams collapse *in the house next door*
he hears slates crash through the eaves *in the house next door*
he hears glass fall from window frames *in the house next
door*
he hears stairs collapse, a bath rust and drop like a bomb
into the cellar *in the house next door*
cries of 'Help, help!' *in the house next door*.
He puts his head under the bedclothes and begins to snore.

Lying in bed,
he hears rain washing through the broken floors
till there isn't a house next door anymore.

Lying in bed,
he hears the crack widen on the side of his house where
the house next door was
no house next door now,

and he hears beams collapse *no house next door now*
slates slide *no house next door now*
and he hears beams collapse *no house next door now*
a chimney breast crumble *no house next door now*
stairs collapse *no house next door now*
and his bed begins to slide through his rotten floor
and he cries 'Help, help!'
But there is no answer from the house next door.

Tony Connor

KON IN SPRINGTIME

The Russian landlord who lets next door's
once carefully cared-for rooms to any-
body, is angry about the money
that's gone from his desk. He doesn't mind whores,
or coloured students, or jailbirds,
or kids. He trails to the 'bins in a tatty
dressing gown, – up at seven thirty
shaking his aristocratic head.

at the evil in men. I like sharing the
area with him; Revolution,
pogroms, years in a Concentration
Camp, haven't made him despair
of human nature. He won't call the police
(he never does), or tell the suspect
to get his paper-baggage packed –
and he isn't Liberal-Minded. He'll curse

rotten the dirty bastard who
robbed him, and make life unpleasant
deliberately, for all his tenants
for at least a day, and perhaps two.
But can't for long not carry his years
gaily: the bow-tie and the collar
of astrakhan are popular
sights in every local bar,

and at sixty-three, it's said, he still
has charm to enjoy the guarded virtue
of good wives, who open their legs to
nothing else that's not legal.
May I survive a barbarous age
as well! Muttering and miming punches,
under a clear blue sky he crunches
back to the door across the spillage

of cinders from his pail. I watch
from the kitchen window, where I've sat
all night, struggling to be a poet
in mid-journey at masterful stretch
among the rich imperatives
of family life. The Russian pauses,
staring at me as though my house is
haunted – reluctant to believe

I'm up at such an hour. He comes
worriedly to the window, certain
I must be awake because of children:
'Is it bad-sick – your little ones?'
he asks. I reassure him – they
vomited but are asleep again.
He beams, who has never heard of Pushkin,
and says 'It will be a lovely day.'

Derek Telling

SONG OF RUINED WORLD

I will build a house for you
out of the wreckage of burst bombs,
imperfect songs, cracked statues,
last will and testaments, politicals
with crowds in their throats.

A house full of last embracing
goodbye words, full of the starvation
of loving hands, millionaires bank rolls
and victory scrolls, dried breasts,
polluted chests and a final suicide note.

In this house will we live
and spend our passion.

I will understand if you think
it is not good enough.

Christopher Logue

CITIZEN'S PROFIT

Let each citizen take note:
Angry blood shows through,
Those who make a profit make
That profit out of you.